Old NEWMILNS

by

Hugh Maxwell

This is one of the oldest surviving prints of Newmilns and shows Greenside in 1845. Loudoun Parish Church had just been rebuilt the previous year, replacing a much older church dating back to 1738 which stood on the same site. A monument in the form of an obelisk was unveiled in 1913 within the church grounds to honour and commemorate the ten men who were killed within Loudoun Parish during the Covenanting struggles. To the left of the church is the old parish school which opened in 1781 and continued in use until 1872. Pupils were taught to read, write and count as well as receiving lessons in Latin, Greek and French. The last schoolmaster was John Lyon Campbell. The bridge giving access over the River Irvine into the Browns Road and the Lanfine Estate is in the background; it was built in the early nineteenth century.

First published in the United Kingdom, 2001,
by Stenlake Publishing, Ochiltree Sawmill, The Lade,
Ochiltree, Ayrshire, KA18 2NX
Telephone/Fax: 01290 423114
enquiries@stenlake.co.uk
www.stenlake.co.uk

ISBN 1 84033 142 9

SOME FURTHER READING

The books listed below were used by the author during his research. None of them are available from Stenlake Publishing. Those interested in finding out more are advised to contact their local bookshop or reference library.

James Mair, *Pictorial History of Newmilns*, 1988.
James Mair, A *Community Rent Asunder*, 1999.
Newmilns and Greenholm Community Council, *Historical Aspects of Newmilns*, 1990.
John Strawhorn, *Ayrshire – The Story of a County*, 1975.
Copies of *The Weekly Supplement and Advertiser* and the *Irvine Valley News* held within the Dick Institute, Kilmarnock.

ACKNOWLEDGEMENTS

The author wishes to thank the staff of the reference department at the Dick Institute, Kilmarnock, and also the many people of Newmilns who were willing to contribute information towards this book. The publishers wish to thank Stanley Zimmer for providing most of the pictures in this book.

The bandstand was located in Greenholm, opposite the bowling green in Nelson Street which can be seen in the background of this photograph. It was erected at the turn of the century when the village was prospering both economically and socially and was a beautiful structure of decorative ironwork and glass. However, its exposed siting proved unpopular with the town's residents and it was used less and less, becoming sadly neglected. In 1908 a white elephant was placed atop the spire of the bandstand as an indication of its unpopularity; it was eventually removed by the burgh council after young boys had spent all day throwing stones at it from Kilnholm Street across the river. Complaints were later received from several residents of the town regarding the bandstand's condition and eventually it was dismantled. All that can be seen today are the iron railings and wall that once surrounded it next to the river.

INTRODUCTION

The town of Newmilns is located within the narrowest part of the Irvine Valley at what was once an ancient fording place across the River Irvine. Around the thirteenth century the valley formed part of an important trade route between the east and west coasts and a small community established itself at the ford where travellers and merchants would often stop to rest and seek shelter.

Within the parish of Loudoun improvements in agriculture were also being developed and local farmers began to require the means for grinding their corn. This narrow area of the Irvine Valley afforded an opportunity to exploit the power of the fast flowing water and several corn and waulk mills were built here. The residents of the surrounding land and also the tenants of the old ferm touns were required or 'thirled' to use these new mills by the landowners and the area became known as 'New Mylls' or 'New Mylnes', terms which were later adapted into the town's modern name.

In 1490 'Newmyllis' was officially created a Free Burgh of Barony in a charter granted by King James IV. This act made the hamlet the fifth burgh within Ayrshire as well as the county's first inland burgh, but more importantly it gave the inhabitants the power and liberty to buy and sell goods such as wines, wax, and woollen and linen cloths. Bakers, brewers, fleshers and other craftsmen could now hold markets to sell and trade their products. A further charter was granted in 1566 by Mary, Queen of Scots which gave the burgh the right to hold its own court and it also later became a Burgh of Regality in 1707.

In the seventeenth century Newmilns became a stronghold of the Covenanting cause. Many local people openly protested against the introduction of an Episcopalian system of church government which was seen as an attempt to extend the beliefs of the Anglican church within Scotland, and they held secret illegal coventicles at surrounding farms. During these troubled times the Keep in Castle Street was used as a prison and to garrison troops who brutally inflicted military repression upon the inhabitants of the town.

Linen weaving was introduced into the village in the 1730s and later some silk, but by the end of the eighteenth century cotton weaving had become established and soon the Irvine Valley became one of the most important handloom weaving areas in the country. A major factor in the development of the industry at that time was the settlement of Flemish and Huguenot immigrants in the village who brought with them the knowledge of how to pattern weave and read the cloth.

During this period the town occupied only a small area with houses on Main Street, Greenside and at the West and East Strands. In 1791 there were 241 male and 25 female weavers within a total population of 1,000. Fifty years later the population had almost doubled to around 1,988 and by then everyone was dependent in some way upon handloom weaving for their existence. In 1841 there were 460 male weavers, 90 female weavers, 230 clippers, 154 winders of pirns as well as wrights, warpers, starchers, mounters, twisters, agents and manufacturers.

This success meant that further housing was needed and in 1872 the town expanded very quickly into Greenholm, an area across the River Irvine in what was actually Galston Parish. This now created the much larger burgh of Newmilns and Greenholm. Streets such as Kilnholm, Union, King, High and Drygate Street were all created around this time. During this prosperous period Joseph Hood, a local man, established himself as a loom builder and engineer. He was responsible for introducing the first jacquard machine to the district and soon all the weavers both in Newmilns and all the neighbouring villages were keen to purchase one of these new looms. The jacquard loom was revolutionary because it obviated the need for draw-boys to create the pattern within the cloth through drawing the strings. The superior quality of the products which were produced by these looms resulted in this type of weaving surviving until 1877, although by that time the number of handloom weavers was beginning to drop and many were forced to leave the town to seek employment elsewhere.

In 1877 Hood introduced the first powerloom lace machine to the town. The powerloom was able to manufacture lace, chenille and madras textiles much more quickly, in greater quantities, and at a cheaper overall cost than the traditional methods. The new industry grew in leaps and bounds, quickly bringing great prosperity and also much needed employment. By 1891 eight large powerloom machine factories had been built in Greenholm and the population had risen to nearly 4,000. A further six large mills were built by 1915 and many natives of the town returned to find employment as weavers, winders, twisters, spoolers, shuttlers and cardmen. In that year the population reached a peak of almost 5,000.

This tremendous industrial success and expansion also resulted in much house building and the prosperity of the town was reflected in the many fine villa style houses that were built for the owners, partners and agents within the lace industry.

After the First World War the lace industry began to face the introduction of tariffs, increasing competition, and recessions both at home and abroad. The golden boom years of the industry were now past and it began to gradually decline. During the Second World War production was switched to the manufacture of blast protective netting and mosquito netting for military use. However, there were now only thirteen factories in operation, nine producing lace, one producing madras and three producing both. Combined, these employed only 1,200 people. The largest at this time was Morton, Young and Borland Ltd who employed 250 people at their lace and madras mill in Greenholm.

Since local councils were replaced by regional councils in 1975 (at which time the Burgh of Newmilns and Greenholm became simply the town of Newmilns) diversification into fabrics woven with acrylic or polyester has enabled the weaving tradition to survive, but by the 1980s there were only six lace and madras factories still working. Today there still seems to be a demand for the again fashionable lace, but only remnants remain of a once hugely successful industry. Many of the factories have closed down, although their sites have been quickly swallowed up by private housing or have become the sites of new business ventures.

Today the population stands at around 3,400. Although many changes have occurred, and most local people are now employed outside the town, there is still great pride and interest in Newmilns' heritage and efforts are being made to preserve it for future generations. The old burgh's motto was 'Weave Truth with Trust' and this still holds true when people remember the remarkable history of old Newmilns and Greenholm.

The east end of Main Street around 1895, looking eastwards from Clark's Pend. The Crown Hotel is on the right, located just before the projecting gable of Auld's Dairy. According to *The Weekly Supplement and Advertiser* of 25 May 1894, 'at about six o'clock in the evening a fire broke out in the stable loft of the Crown Hotel. . . . The fire brigade proceeded at once to the spot and with the excellent supply of water in the mains the hose was speedily brought into play. One who failed in directing the nozzle towards the flames had his breast and neck batted in the deluge. This cooled his ardour and the nozzle was quickly passed into safer hands. The brigade quickly confined the flames to the shed and in about half an hour the fire proper was subdued. Damage done was confined to five tons of hay and one ton of straw, all being insured. The roof of the building was also demolished.' The cause of the fire was unknown. In 1927 the proprietor of the Crown Hotel became Mrs Cummings and it became renowned locally as the place to go for lunches and teas. It continues to be popular with locals today.

The Morton Hall was built of red sandstone in 1896 and provided seating for 1,000 people. It was gifted to the town by William Morton, one of the town's most noted benefactors. In 1908 *The Weekly Supplement and Advertiser* reported that 'very strange, weird-like noises have been heard of late emanating from the Morton Hall. To those doing business in the Committee Rooms it sounded as if the witches in Macbeth were holding high revel, or as if Edgar Allen Poe's raven had returned to croak. Let us proceed to allay the fears of the nervous. The cause is none of these things. It is the Newmilns Amateur Operatic and Dramatic Society in their rehearsals of 'Our Regiment' which raises the din! The first performance of Hamilton's military comedy is billed for New Year's Day and the desire of the historic amateur is to be 'business' and letter perfect. It is a commendable desire!'.

The Joseph Hood drinking fountain at the front of Mr Rawlinson's hotel (now the Bridgend Bar), Main Street, *c.*1895. It was gifted by the Provost Joseph Hood (he held this position on several occasions) and marked the installation of a gravitational water system within the town. According to *The Weekly Supplement and Advertiser* in April 1894 the fountain was the scene of a practical joke: 'Strong drink is an insinuating curse and the firmest have cause to tremble at its menaces. Though we have lately been accustomed to seeing unperpendicular figures staggering through our streets the sight of the Joseph Hood fountain upon the fuddle was most dreadful. Undoubtedly the trick was played by the nightshift boys, one of whom climbed up the central column and placed a bottle upon the topmost spike of the structure, neck downwards, which was suggestive. It looked like a whisky bottle but maybe it was only a vinegar bottle in which someone had preserved cold-tea to allay the thirst of the night watch. Whoever the culprit is, we hope he completed the farce by tumbling into the waters beneath and we are sure the cold would fly to his weakest part!'

The Wincey Mill in Greenholm pictured around the 1880s. It was built to manufacture a mixture of cotton warp and woollen weft known as 'wincey goods' (wincey was the name given to the material). It preceded all the other large lace and madras factories that would be erected later in Greenholm. In 1876 Joseph Hood, at that time a mechanic, and Hugh Morton, a weaving agent, installed the first steam-powered lace machine within this mill. There were also several other special machines within the factory patented by Hood. One of these was a doubling or spinning machine for doubling some of the yarns. Its purpose was to put a twist on figured chenille so that it would always be a given length and thus when woven the pattern would be 'set' with the least amount of trouble. This is the view looking eastwards towards the centre of the town. The mill was later extended and used to manufacture lace, madras, chenille and tapestry. Owned by Hood, Morton and Co. it is one of the few mills in the town still in operation.

This photograph taken in the early 1890s shows the many large lace mills that were built across the river in Greenholm and which heralded the explosion of the machine lace industry within the town. In the foreground can be seen the Lanfine Bleaching and Finishing Works of Messrs Forrest, Gillies and Co. (built in 1883). About sixty people were employed here where lace goods were brought fresh off the loom to be washed, bleached and finished ready for the marketplace. It closed in 1932 but is remembered for having the tallest chimney of all the factories in the town. Also to be seen are the Caledonian Lace Works of Messrs A. and J. Muir (built 1885) where a hundred people were employed at the looms which were powered by an engine of 75 horsepower, and the Annbank Lace Works of Robert Muir and Son (built 1882) which employed about 130 people with the machines also driven by an engine of 75 horsepower.

One of the large powerloom lace machines with a Jacquard overhead that could be found within many of the Newmilns factories around the early 1900s. The machines often reached lengths of over thirty feet and a curtain of that width could have been woven, although more usually (as in this picture) four curtains were woven at the one time. The machine worked on the following very simplified principle. The warp was stretched perpendicularly all along the loom and came down between two horizontal iron bars that carried the shuttles. The round brass shuttles or bobbins allowed the warp to pass through but as they oscillated backwards and forwards the thread became woven round them due to the action of steel points and formed the cloth that was the basis of the lace. The pattern, which was the real beauty of the material, was formed by another set of threads that came from 'spools' placed on a board behind the machine and their action in forming the pattern was controlled by the jacquard that rose about twenty feet above the loom. In this photograph the lace weaver is working the centre wheel that was used to stop and balance the loom while in front of him is the catchbar handle.

Pictured in 1895 is the rear of the old Loudoun Manse on St Margaret's Hill where Robert Burns slept in the room with the window on the left marked by a cross. Burns was a frequent visitor to the Rev. George Lawrie at the manse where he enjoyed the warm family hospitality and spent many nights singing and dancing. A compliment to the minister's wife was etched by Burns with the stone of his ring onto the window's glass: 'Lovely Mrs Lawrie, she is all charms'. Rev. Lawrie was instrumental in changing Burns' mind about emigrating to the West Indies and persuaded him to stay in Scotland. Unfortunately, the glass was cracked during an exhibition in 1949 held to mark the Civic Week, but the window is now on display at the Dick Institute, Kilmarnock. The old manse still stands and is currently being restored by its present owners.

The old Loudoun Meal Mill was located on the banks of the River Irvine at Ladeside near the Townhead. It had been used for grinding corn since the seventeenth century and was owned by the Loudoun family until the early 1900s. It finally ceased production in the 1960s, with the water wheel being removed ten years later. The mill itself has now been transformed into a private house although the words 'No Mill, No Meal' can still be seen painted on the mill wall. The lade for the mill ran from the dam located slightly further upstream. Just out of picture on the right were the old stepping stones that were used to cross the water. They were washed away and replaced by the Mill Steps Bridge in 1928.

Newmilns and Greenholm pictured in 1899 from the top of the Craig. In the foreground can be seen the road leading up towards the Tilework Bridge and Mount Pleasant Farm while on the left of the picture was 'Bedlam', the local nickname for Stewart's Place. Within the town itself can be seen the Greenholm Bridge and on the far right are the Co-operative buildings and the drinking fountain at the Brigend corner. The old gas works chimney in 'The Wilderness' behind the Co-op is also visible while Jacob's Ladder can be seen climbing up towards Loudoun Crescent.

The Institute Brig on the left gave access from Craigview Road over the river onto the Browns Road which was a popular walk linking Newmilns with Darvel. Near the bridge and the steps is the old parish school and schoolhouse, and adjacent to this is the 'Beadle's House' at the corner of East Strand and the old cemetery wall of the parish kirk. The man is walking over the strong wooden bridge that was erected over the Noral Burn to replace a much older stone bridge. The photograph dates from the early 1900s; the river banks were also repaired at this time and several seats were placed on the Green for the convenience of the public.

Townhead, looking west along Main Street, around 1905. Right of centre, at the junction of Back Street, is the Townhead Athletic Bar, known informally by the locals as the Angel Inn. Across the road is the Crown Hotel. An advertisement within *The Weekly Supplement and Advertiser* at this time informed readers that at the Townhead were the premises of John Grant, coachbuilder: 'Coachmaking in all its branches undertaken on the premises. Every requisite of the trade kept in stock. Repairs, painting and trimming promptly attended to. Polo carts, dog carts and market carts of the latest designs. Leading features include the quality of material and workmanship combined with moderate prices.'

Councillors standing in front of the Morton Hall. On 13 July, 1894, many councillors took part in the ceremony of 'Cutting the Burgh Peats'. They gathered in Main Street from where they proceeded to Loudoun Moor and performed the annual ceremony of cutting peat, a right which they had held since the charter of 1566. On this occasion they proceeded to West Heads Farmhouse and the road leading to the edge of the moor. A small audience had assembled and after reading from the old charter, William Steel, Chancellor of the council, proceeded to cut a peat in the name of the burgh and its inhabitants. Three hearty cheers were given to the memory of those past, songs were sung, and an enjoyable hour was spent by all in attendance.

Children standing at Mitchell's Corner between High Street and King Street. The entrance to the new public school was on the left. In September 1908 *The Weekly Supplement and Advertiser* contained a delightful little story regarding 'The Needle': 'Whether it be sewing, packing or drawing, the needle is an indispensable adjunct of modern civilisation. This is not a technical article on these tiny steel tools which always sparkle like a locomotive engine newly come from the shop. It is merely a harmless little story which, through its sheer veracity, may raise the smile incredulous. This precocious little youth of five seasons from Newmilns, who had been in the habit of doing some of the errands to the store, for his maternal parent, was dispatched to a haberdasher's in Main Street for a packet of sewing needles. "What size?" queried the lady at the counter. The youth hesitated not a jot and said "745". The lady smiled inaudibly. The boy was unacquainted with eight betweens but he was closely cognisant of his store number. He got the needles!'

In 1894 the new public school was opened on an elevated position just off High Street. The school became known as 'Hood's School' after Archibald Hood who was its headmaster for forty years. By 1951 the school had 503 pupils with children from the Gilfoot and Masons Holm area travelling in by bus. At that time around 140 of the pupils also took part in the school's football and net-ball teams. The bell was added into the tower sometime after it was opened and many of the town's residents will recall the ringing that signalled 'hame time' or 'schules oot'. Unfortunately, in 1960 the school was damaged beyond repair by fire and today pupils are now sent to Loudoun Academy near Galston for their secondary education.

The old Council House located at the Cross was built in 1739 and has long been at the centre of the town's civic activity. It was built by the fourth Earl of Loudoun to house the town council of the Burgh of Barony. It has a belfry and a tower as well as a double outside stair whose landing makes an ideal platform from which to address an open-air crowd. Many a rousing oration has been delivered from here. The bell in the tower greatly predates the building and is engraved with the date 1547, although its origin is unknown. The upstairs was used as a court and council chamber while the lower storey was a tolbooth for the 'imprisonment and warding of delinquents and other vagrants'. A list of cases heard at the court on one day in July 1895 gives an insight into its business: Jeanie Aird of Isles Street was fined the sum of five shillings for being drunk and incapable; for throwing stones at and maliciously breaking telegraph cups on the Darvel Road, Henry Bowie of Union Street and John Aneell of Main Street were given the choice of a 2/6 fine or 24 hours imprisonment; a trio of boys from the High Street were also charged with the theft of strawberries from a garden there, but were allowed to go after being severely reprimanded.

In June 1895 *The Weekly Supplement and Advertiser* reported that 'the small remnant of the handloom weavers left within the town was constantly on the decrease and although the total number of them does not amount to more than about thirty or forty now, yet even they cannot find employment. At present nearly all of them are idle and they may be seen wiling away the time about the streets, or standing in groups discussing the latest questions or mourning over the days that are past when the shuttle went whizzing merrily through the loom and the whir of the pirn-wheel was heard at nearly every door. The day of the handloom weaving industry is gone and it will die out in Newmilns when the present generation of weavers has passed away'.

The town's last handloom weaver had ceased work in 1906. In this scene some men, probably ex-weavers, have gathered to watch the Joseph Hood fountain being cleaned outside the Brigend Inn at the 'Fuddle' (as this area of town used to be known).

Pictured in Brown Street at the turn of the century is the rag and bone man with his donkey and cart, complete with scales. This sight was known locally as 'Bonny Robert and his Cuddy' and Robert was typical of the many characters that could be found within the town at this time. In the background can be seen one of the water pumps that were erected in the street after the installation of the gravitational water system. A letter to *The Weekly Supplement and Advertiser* in March 1890 informed readers: 'Now that the Commissioners have got the gravitation water at our doors, it is their duty now to see that it is not abused by a number of mischievous boys. I do not know how other parts of the town fare in this respect, but I know that in Brown Street the waste of water extracted for malicious purposes, almost constantly, is quite an unbearable spectacle, by turning it on and spouting it all roads, much to the inconvenience of those passing by and not only that, but the footpath in front of those houses where the pumps are set down are being converted into perfect mud holes which cannot long be tolerated by the proprietors!'

The railway reached Newmilns in 1850. The first station was replaced by a larger one in 1890 to cater for the huge influx of workers and the factories receiving raw materials and dispatching their finished goods. In July 1890 *The Weekly Supplement and Advertiser* reported: 'The new Glasgow & South Western Railway passenger station, which has been in the process of construction for a long time was opened for traffic on Tuesday. The premises are handsome, commodious and well fitted up with the most modern conveniences. . . . They comprise booking office, agent's room, general waiting room, gentlemen's first class waiting room and ladies first class waiting room with stationmaster's dwelling house.' In this photograph can be seen the large goods shed and platform, with the actual station and footbridge just out of picture on the right. From right to left can also be seen the lace mills of Haddow, Aird and Crerar (built 1881), the Irvine Bank Lace Factory of William Morton and Co. (built 1879), the Ayrshire Lace Works of Stewart, Moir and Muir Ltd (built 1880) and the Vale Lace Works of Johnstone, Shields and Co. (built 1880). The railway closed in the early 1960s and the site is now occupied by the Vesuvius Crucible Company.

The interior of a typical Newmilns lace mill of the early 1900s. The weavers and spoolers can be seen standing at the end of their looms which were used to manufacture lace curtains. The machines were powered by dangerous overhead belt driven pulleys. On the right are the shuttling tables. At their Irvine Bank Factory, Messrs David Ligat and Son manufactured lappet and muslin fabrics. One hundred and twenty people manufactured the light, filmy looking figured fabric known as 'lappet', which was used only to a limited extent in this country for window screens and other light draping purposes. It was mostly exported to the East for making turbans and other articles of dress and lappet shawls were also woven for use in Persia and India.

A fire at the Co-operative Society's central premises started at five o'clock in the morning of 14 June, 1908. It started within the drapery department and soon turned it into a seething mass of flames. When the fire brigade arrived the fire already had a thorough grip of the building and was spreading rapidly. Fortunately little or no wind was blowing but the danger to adjoining properties was considerable. So intense was the heat that at Cuthbertson's property opposite, the paint on the face of the wall was almost completely blistered off and many panes of glass were cracked and broken. The fire brigade tried hard to save the building but it was entirely gutted. The damage done was estimated to be around £8,000.

This photograph taken around 1900 shows Kilnholm Street looking west into Loudoun Road. The old iron brig is visible spanning the river and linking Nelson Street with Loudoun Road. It gave access for workers to the mills in Greenholm. On the right are the distinctive 'Glesca Buildings', known as this due to their similarity to the tenements of Glasgow. In September 1908, *The Weekly Supplement and Advertiser* reported that 'road making' was being carried out here. 'The road roller which by its weight and skill is earnestly doing its best for the condition of the roads met with a rude shock to its feelings which threatened to incapacitate it from active duty for some time. Whilst rolling in Kilnholm Street, the old arching of the culvert of the Caffle Burn gave way, and one of the side wheels was precipitated into the burn. For some time it was in a precarious state and did not look well, but a steady application of labour put it on its feet after a lapse of seven hours. It reached home shortly after six somewhat pale and nervous, but not a whit the worse of its accident!'

The Strath Dam on the River Irvine was located at Mason's Holm and was a popular destination for walkers from both Newmilns and Galston. A lade ran from the dam to power the old Strath paper mill. There is little water flowing down the actual dam because the lade was also used to power the Barr corn mill and the old saw mill at Kilknowe for cutting timber. Strath Mill itself dates back to 1639 and was latterly involved in producing pattern cards for the jacquard machines within the lace industry. It was also where John Macintosh had his studio. He was responsible for designing many of the local buildings, including the new public school, and was also a renowned local photographer. The lade itself can be seen on the right of the picture while a cart is heading in the direction of the town loaded with bags of meal. Sadly the dam was washed away in the floods of 1920 and all that remains of the Strath Mill today is part of the original cottage.

This is the view taken from the top of Jacob's Ladder looking southeast over the town towards Lanfine in 1905. Loudoun Parish Church is distinctive on the left with its clock face and spire while the large viaduct built over the river can also be seen stretching through the town, taking the railway up to Darvel. The central premises of the Co-operative Society are visible at the corner of Main Street and Doitburn Road, while in the foreground the river looks as though it has almost run dry. On the right the Royal Bank building in Brown Street is visible, as are the old handloom cottages on Nelson Street (foreground right). To the left of the Loudon Parish Church can be seen the Keep and the lace factory of Messrs Henderson, Morton and Inglis at the bottom of the Darvel Road.

In 1927 an advertisement for the Newmilns Co-operative Society Ltd read: 'We can supply all the needs of our resident members and also visitors with the finest value in best class groceries, provisions, bread, fleshing, coal, drapery, boots, furnishing and hardware all at keen competitive prices. Discounts of 2/- in the pound allowed on all purchases to non-members. Goods delivered to all parts of the town. Central premises and offices – Main Street, Newmilns, also at No.1 branch, King Street and No.2 branch, Jamieson Terrace.' Pictured here in 1914, the impressive facade of the Co-operative buildings was completely restored following the disastrous fire of 1908. By 1950 the society had over 1,508 members and was the largest retail business within the town. A chemist's shop was also operated by the Scottish Co-operative Wholesale Society. Today the building is again a shell after another fire, but plans are being undertaken to restore the building to its former condition.

Nelson Street in Greenholm was known locally as the 'Water Wynd'. In the foreground is the River Irvine with the Greenholm Bridge on the left, while dominating the background is the Craig with the road winding up towards Mount Pleasant. The Royal Bank building in Brown Street is distinctive on the left with its unusually shaped rooftop. It was built around 1890 for the Mitchell family of Johnstone Shields Ltd, and was modelled on Brodick Castle on the Isle of Arran. Within it is a large staircase overlooked by five stained glass windows bearing the images of the Scottish poets Robert Burns, Sir Walter Scott, Alan Ramsay, Robert Tannahill and James Hogg. Today little has changed in this scene, although the Craig is now covered with woodland.

Children playing on the 'Miller's Dam' which was located between the Institute Brig and the Greenholm Bridge. The song 'Lang, Lang Syne' by the Rev. George Lawrie describes how the children used to spoil the curling that was often played here during the winter when the water was completely frozen over: 'Do ye mind the miller's dam/ When the frosty winter cam'/ Hoo we slade alang the curlers' rinks/ And made their game a sham;/ When they chased us through the snaw/ We took leg-bail ane an' a/ But we did it o'er again in the mornin?' The dam was used by Pate's Mill in Greenholm. The sluice was just out of picture on the left and it filled the lade which ran behind the houses on the south side of Brown Street. The dam was washed away in the 'Lammas floods' of the 1920s and the mill itself was demolished in 1977.

Brown Street in Greenholm, looking eastwards towards the Brigend corner. The photograph was taken from just over the bridge for Pate's Mill lade where the man on the right can be seen standing. In June 1895 *The Weekly Supplement and Advertiser* reported: 'Runaway horse – on Monday at the dinner-hour, a horse yoked to the baker's van of the Co-operative Society bolted while coming up Brown Street. In spite of the utmost efforts of the driver to control it, the animal continued its course till, when rounding the corner at the Joseph Hood fountain, the van fell over on its side. The driver was thrown off rather roughly, and received some bad cuts about the face, but beyond this no other damage was done!' Some of the businesses on Brown Street included Morton the blacksmith, Muir the blacksmith, Torrance the grocer, Wallace and Torrance the joiners and cabinet makers, Alexander Mathie the newsagent and J. Kirkland the coal merchant.

The view from the Craig, 1934. Looking northwards, the new public school overlooks the town while High Street can be seen winding its way eastwards up towards the cemetery at the Dalwhatswood Plantation where there was also once a smallpox hospital. The rear of the houses in Main Street and at the Cross can also be seen with the distinctive rooftop of the Keep visible in the centre. This fortified tower house in Castle Street is the oldest building within the town, dating back to the sixteenth century. It was originally occupied by the Loudoun family up until early in the seventeenth century, but is more widely known for its role in the town's Covenanting history. During that period dragoons were garrisoned within it and it was also used as a prison. One night a daring raid was undertaken to rescue eight prisoners destined to be shot the following morning. The guard was shot and the gates were broken with large hammers before the prisoners could escape. Unfortunately one rescuer, John Law, was shot dead by a soldier from within the tower. More recently the Keep has been restored, but after use as a private dwelling it is now empty again.

The extension of the railway from Newmilns up to Darvel in 1896 necessitated the building of the huge 26 arched viaduct spanning the River Irvine and dividing the 'Big Green' in two. In this photograph taken in 1910 can be seen from left to right the Joseph Hood factory chimney on Main Street, the 'Baun Hall' on Greenside which was formerly the beaming shed of the Handloom Weavers Association, and further along the distinctive three-storey building known locally as the 'Barracks'. Above the viaduct the chimney of the Henderson, Morton and Inglis factory in Darvel Road is clearly visible accompanied on its right by that of J. & J. Wilson's Greenhead factory. At this time it was common for the Green to be used by local people for drying their laundry.

Looking west along Main Street towards the Cross, 1923. Outside the premises of M. & W. Walker's newsagents and printing office can be seen a selection of postcards depicting local views. These would have been examples of the popular 'Loudoun Series', many of which appear in this book. Further along past the small grocers shop were the premises of Joseph Hood where he manufactured sewing frames and jacquard machines, and also later produced appliances for the lace machines. Twenty-four people were employed here within the workshop where the 'harness' boards for the lace looms were skilfully manufactured. Even though each board was just a yard in length with a width of 2⅜ inches, they required between 1,400 to 4,400 holes to be bored in them. Just past the workshop was the Newmilns Temperance Hotel while across the street are the railings for Lady Flora's Institute adjacent to the Morton Hall.

Lady Flora Elizabeth Hastings, daughter of the first Marquess of Hastings and a member of the Loudoun family, was appointed Lady of the Bedchamber to the Duchess of Kent, the mother of Queen Victoria. A cruel and unfounded slander was circulated within the Queen's court that she was pregnant when in fact she had an infected liver with severe intestinal complications, resulting in her swollen appearance. This condition resulted in her death at Buckingham Palace in 1839 amid much public scandal and outcry against Queen Victoria. She was a gifted poet and a volume of her poems was edited and published by her sister, the Marchioness of Bute. It raised £700 and this was further supplemented by a bequest of £12,000 from the Marchioness herself. Financed by this money, the school was erected as a memorial to her sister and opened in September 1877, providing much needed education for girls as well as giving the town one of its most attractive buildings. It catered for 200 girls and there were only three headmistresses until 1919 when all pupils were transferred to the new public school. It later reopened as a Women's Institute in 1921, but finally closed in 1981 after which it fell into serious disrepair. Today, it has been restored to its former magnificence and is in use as a retirement home for the elderly people of the town.

The view east along the Main Street from the corner of the East Strand, 1907. On the right are the railings of the parish church followed by the pole for Gemmell's barber shop. On the left can be seen Semple's the fruiterer, the entry to Mr Oliver the dentist who was upstairs, Mitchell's shoe shop, John Loudoun's bakery and then the Commercial Hotel which was later renamed the Covenanter's Hotel. The Morton Hall is next door and the trees mark the grounds of Lady Flora's School. The houses on the right were demolished in the 1960s and replaced by council housing, while across the street several of the older buildings have disappeared altogether. Another Main Street business many people will recall is the Rex Cinema, which was built on the site of the old Cross Keys Inn. Seating 750, it opened in 1939 and quickly became the Irvine Valley's premier picture theatre for an evening's good entertainment. Sadly, it closed in 1986.

This is the view at the foot of the 'Cut' in Darvel Road looking west into Isles Street at the Townhead. On the left is the lace factory of Henderson, Morton and Inglis built in 1898, while in Isles Street the local smiddy can be seen at the corner of Burn Road. Across the road a cyclist is standing at the entrance to Campbell Street; the photographer himself is standing adjacent to Mill Road. This gave access under the railway bridge down past the Townhead Farm to Loudoun Mill and the cottages on Ladeside. The scene has changed greatly: the factory building was demolished after it was rendered unsafe by fire while on the right the villas still remain, but past the junction to Campbell Street all the old houses have been replaced by council housing. In 1954 the town 'coup' was washed down into the Darvel Road and totally engulfed all this area.

Main Street, looking east towards the Cross. On the left a delivery lorry from Turner and Ewing is parked outside the Burns Tavern and the Loudoun Arms. According to the *New Statistical Account of* 1842 there were fourteen publicans and fifteen licensed grocers within the town which resulted in a large quantity of whisky being drunk especially by the working class and those suffering from the effects of poverty – 'The weaver after sitting sixteen hours a day in a damp loom-shop without healthy bodily exercise, his nerves unstrung, his digestive organs deranged, will often rob himself of his food and raiment to banish, by intoxification, that bodily wretchedness and mental irritability which he knows from sad experience, will soon return with increased misery. The habit of drinking is thus often formed, and, when once formed, never almost is it banished. Much whisky is also consumed in our village by a class of weavers called trampers, generally young men, who live miserably, spending the greater portion of their wages on whisky, which they consume, not only in public and private houses, but also out in the fields.'

The father-in-law of Robert Burns, James Armour of Mauchline, was contracted to build the central part of Lanfine House between 1769 and 1772. John Brown, a textile manufacturer and banker within the city of Glasgow was the original owner of the house. He was also a bailie and gained enough wealth to buy the original land upon which the house itself is built. The policies were planted with many beautiful trees and shrubs and three gatehouses were also built to give access. Successive lairds continually improved both the house and the estate until it grew to over 37,000 acres. Although today the estate is much reduced in size, it is currently up for sale at a price tag of £3,000,000. Local people still enjoy the pleasant tree-lined walks throughout the estate. At one time there were many locals employed by the estate as servants, gardeners, foresters and stable-hands. The house itself contains twelve bedrooms, five bathrooms, a large dining room, several smaller sitting rooms and lounges, as well as four staff apartments.

The west gatehouse of the Lanfine Estate with Craigs wood in the background. *The Weekly Supplement and Advertiser* carried a report on the agricultural show at Lanfine, held on Saturday 1 May, 1920: 'The Browns Road was quickly transformed into a busy thoroughfare on Saturday, all roads leading there for Downiesburn Park, Lanfine, where the annual cattle show of the Loudoun and Galston Agricultural Society was held. In the afternoon the attendance would nearly reach the 3,000 mark, which was a record for the show. The programme was very enticing, embracing boy's races, bandsmen's race, pillow fight, display of highland dancing, gymnastics and an exhibition of sheep dog trials. The Stonehouse pipe band rendered selections and a parade of all animals took place at 3 o'clock. In addition to the ordinary prizes, a number of handsome special prizes and medals have been given for competition by local gentlemen!' The cattle show is still held annually at nearby Loudoun Castle.

On 20 August, 1920, flooding of the River Irvine, known locally as the 'Lammas floods', occurred. *The Weekly Supplement and Advertiser* reported: 'It had been estimated that as much rain fell in one day as normally in the whole month. . . . During the night the river became a seething and uncontrollable current, refusing to be limited by its own narrow channel and ultimately gained an opening at all weak parts of its boundaries. Daylight revealed the results which passed all the guessings of human intelligence. The stone wall in Main Street had been unable to stand the pressure, a considerable portion of the wall and roadway being carried off, leaving only as much solid ground in the street as to permit a horse and cart to pass. The damage can only be repaired at a heavy cost. . . . Several of the factories were also damaged such as Messrs Henderson, Inglis and Co. at the Townhead. A lade over which the factory was built burst under the pressure of the water and flooded the interior of the shed, partially immersing the machines. It can be safely said that never before has flooding to such an extent taken place, and no one who saw it will forget it readily. The Greenside just now is a source of delight to the wee bairns. When the high waters receded, a large quantity of sand was left and here the little ones play. All week it has just been like Ettrick Bay or Saltcoats on sand castle competition day!' In the background is the chimney of the old gas works.

Looking west from Kilnholm Street into Loudoun Road in the early 1920's, shortly after the damage to the road caused by the 'Lammas floods' had been repaired. Instead of replacing the wall along the river's edge it was decided by the Burgh Council to erect railings which are still there today. On the right is Wilson Place with John Mair's Garage followed by the large 'Glesca' buildings that have since been demolished. Further along is 'Baldies Brae' and the bottom of the public right of way called locally the 'Jacobs Ladder'. On the left is the bandstand in the 'Water Wynd' whilst in the background is the 'iron brig' which gave access for the factory workers over the River Irvine to the lace and madras mills in Greenholm. Kilnholm Street takes its name from the limestone workings and their kilns that once existed here.

The 'Iron Brig' was constructed in 1881 to give easier access for the factory workers from Loudoun Road across the river to Nelson Street in Greenholm. It was the first footbridge to be built across the water but was later joined by the Mill Steps Bridge and the one at Masons Holm. Eventually there would be five footbridges in total as well as the two older stone bridges giving access over the water. A large flood in 1954 rendered the 'iron brig' unsafe and it was replaced with a more solid concrete structure. On the left in this picture can be seen the factory building of Hood, Morton and Co., newly rebuilt after destruction by fire.

There was a rich variety of small shops centred around the Cross in Main Street at the time of this 1931 photograph. There was J.H. Greene and Sons, newsagents and printers, where the weekly newspaper the *Irvine Valley News* was published and distributed from, Dewar's the chemist, the Buttercup Dairy Co., and Ronald's the bakers at 26 Main Street where confections, home baked scones and pancakes could be sampled in the tea room. There was also John Smith's the tobacconist at 56 Main Street where all the best brands of cigars, tobaccos and cigarettes were stocked. Special lines (as advertised in the *Newmilns and Greenholm Official Guide* of 1927) included the McCullochs Mixture, a 'fragrant mixture of medium strength', and also the Lanfine Mixture – 'a full satisfying smoke'. John Findlay, watchmaker and jeweller was at 64 Main Street, where everything from engagement and gem rings, fishing tackle, golf requisites and fancy goods could be purchased. J. & N. Coubrough the milliners and ladies and children's outfitters also sold the daintiest of millinery and the most up-to-date styles in hats from their premises in Main Street.

The Brown's Institute in Main Street at the Cross was built by the late Miss Martha Brown of Lanfine who gifted it to the town in 1870. It was established for working men and comprised a public library, reading room and a recreational room. Lectures, concerts, socials and weddings were often held within its walls. Today it is currently being restored to its former condition and in this picture a large group of local working men can be seen standing outside it. Miss Brown later also gifted the ornate drinking fountain that once stood at the Cross. Further along can be seen the premises of Todd's ironmongers and plumbers, followed by the old council house with its tower and bell. Across the street two men are standing at the entrance to Castle Street where the oldest building within the town, the Keep, is located.

In October 1922 a war memorial was unveiled within the grounds of Lady Flora's Institute to the memory of the 138 men who did not return from the First World War. The address and unveiling was performed by the local MP, the Hon. Alexander Shaw, in the presence of a large assembled crowd. After the proceedings a hymn was played by Newmilns Burgh Silver Prize Band. During this a very large number of floral wreaths and bouquets were laid on the steps of the memorial by relatives, friends and others. The service closed with the band playing the national anthem. After the conclusion of the Second World War in 1945 the names of forty men were added to the memorial and a small garden was created which still surrounds the monument today.

The Main Street and Cross, 1950. On the right with the car parked in front are the premises of the Clydesdale Bank (formerly the Black Bull Hotel) followed by the entrance to Castle Street and the Loudoun Arms hotel which was formerly called the Eagle Inn. On the left can be seen the Brown's Institute at the corner of Craigview Road while further along at the Cross are the premises of M. Todd and Co., ironmongers, plumbers, slaters, heating and sanitary engineers. The business was established in 1862 and grew steadily, also becoming the main cycle supplier and repairer within both Newmilns and Darvel. Their shop is still trading from the Cross today.

Main Street captured by the camera in 1931 when the motor car and cycle had almost completely replaced the horse and cart as the favoured mode of transport. However, a few decades earlier in 1890 all the townspeople rushed to the Main Street to gaze in awe at a hitherto unseen spectacle – Mr Bowie of West Overland, one of the most enterprising farmers in the district, delivering potatoes to all the traders in Newmilns from a wagon drawn by a small traction engine. According to *The Weekly Supplement and Advertiser:* 'Children and adults stopped their activity to stand in amazement as hissing, spluttering and puffing was accompanied by smoke, steam and flames! The quantity of potatoes delivered on this occasion was five tons and his employment of this means and saving in consequence of horsepower is creditable to his enterprise. The engine . . . is also employed by him in farm work and in driving his threshing mill.'

Looking westwards along the Darvel Road towards the 'Cut', 1939. With the expansion of the burgh, council and private houses were built at Alstonpapple (formerly called 'Astinpapple'). This area was once a small community separate from Newmilns but with the subsequent building of houses and the expansion of the town it became part of the burgh. The council houses were named Isles Terrace and were built in the 1920s and early 30s to alleviate the shortage of housing for families living within the town. These houses command superb views southwards, looking over the woodland policies of Lanfine Estate. There is little change in this scene today with only the introduction of traffic calming measures on the road itself being obvious.